Amrita Sharma is a young voice with a promise. She plays with colours of defiance, celebrates the anguish, and deals with subjects that reflect the human condition. Her thoughts lead her into a world of possibility.

RANU UNIYAL
Professor
Department of English
and Modern European Languages
University of Lucknow

The Skies

poems

AMRITA SHARMA

Hawakal
PUBLISHERS
New Delhi | Calcutta

HAWAKAL PUBLISHERS PRIVATE LIMITED
70 B/9 Amritpuri, East of Kailash, New Delhi 65
33/1/2 K B Sarani, Mall Road, Calcutta 80

Email info@hawakal.com
Website www.hawakal.com

Cover designed by Bitan Chakraborty

First edition (paperback) July 2022

ISBN: 978-93-91431-10-5 (paperback)

Price: 350 INR | 14.99 USD

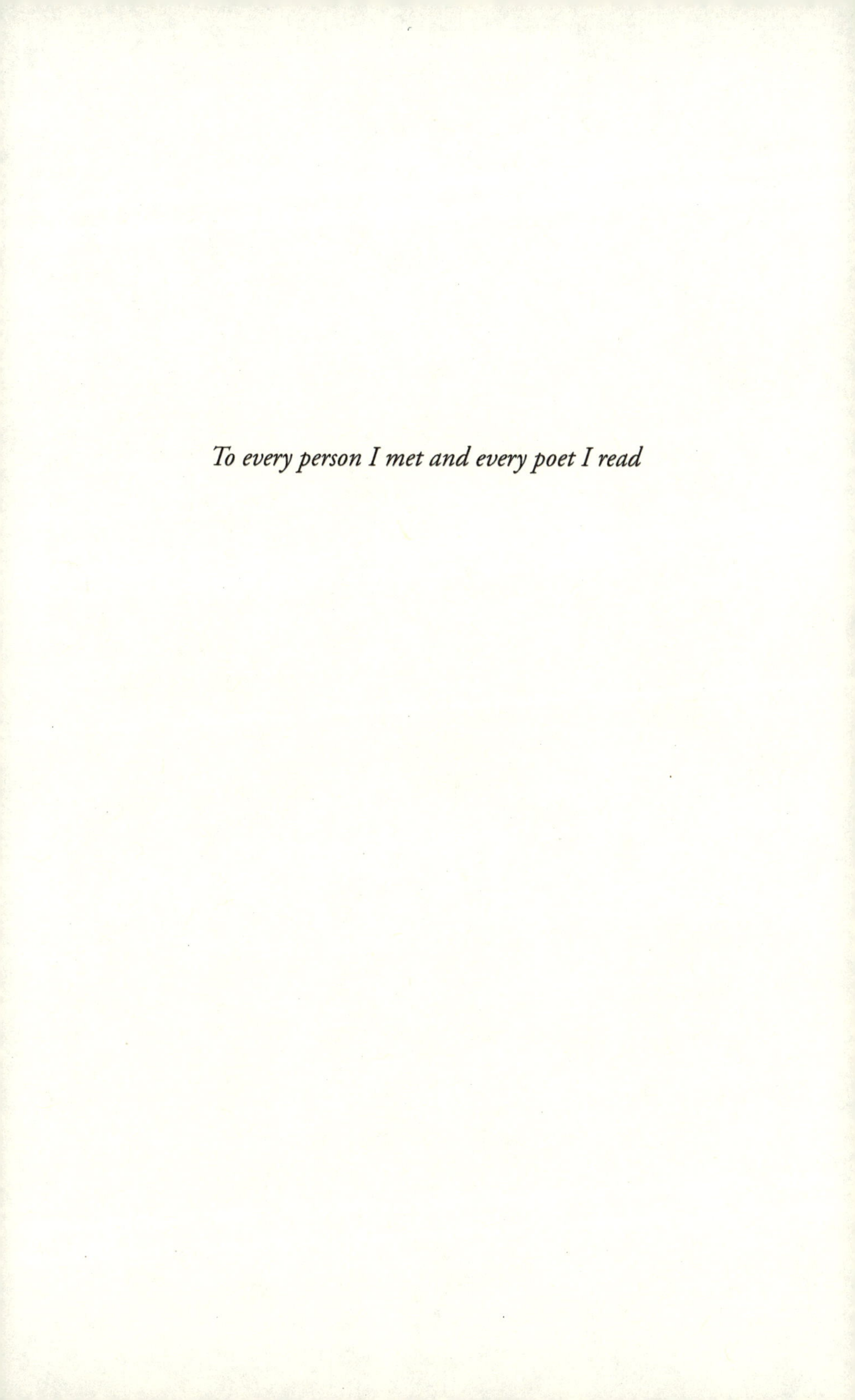

To every person I met and every poet I read

ACKNOWLEDGEMENTS

With no universal conceits, this collection is a collage of personal encounters, narrated in verse. I thank each memory and misery, every critique and companion, every joy and journey, and all that life offered so far.

Several names however stand out. A '*guru*' takes you by hand and leads you on, and I thank Prof. Ranu Uniyal for her blessings and love throughout. To find a poet as a Ph.D. supervisor was an inspiration, to find a mother in a *guru* was a blessing. She remains my guiding light and an endeared source of strength. I dedicate every success so far to her presence and yet believe that no words or actions can ever suffice.

I dearly remember my grandfather Late Shri Murali Dhar Baurai today as my first teacher and the first poet I ever read. He was the first pillar of strength and my family has sustained me thereafter.

I owe many of these writings to a passionate love for poetry that arose out of conversations with fellow poets. During the first wave of the Covid pandemic in India, the quarantine brought me close to many poetic pens, and the subsequent years led to exchange of verses with them, and many of those texts find place in this collection. I cherish that time and poetic discussions, particularly with Prithvi bhaiya and Roopam Di, with their zeal for reading giving fuel to mine.

I also read many Urdu and Hindi poet friends in the past two years that greatly added to my love for this art form. I am thankful to all of these poet friends who were a constant reader for me. I particularly thank Niranjan Kumar, a friend I never met in person, and yet whose writings influenced me the most.

Most of these poems were written in India, however, a substantial part was also written during my term as a Hindi Fulbright faculty in the United States. Many of the people I met there have a recurrent presence in many of these poems. I lovingly acknowledge Sunyoung from South Korea, whom I refer as "*Unni*" or elder sister in one of the poems here. Osama from Egypt remains my best friend from the time and an inevitable part of my writings from Notre Dame.

The best of friends are also the strongest critics of our work, and I owe many hours of poetic discussions and debates to Ahmed Shams, a colleague in US from Bangladesh, and my dearest critic so far. I believe his insights on poetry brought me closer to conflicts and corrections within me and my work.

I am still exploring my love for poetry and I thank *Hawakal* for bringing my poems to print.

CONTENTS

Musings

THE SKIES

In singularities of space and ground,
in canary hues and crimson tinge,
our skies appear so strange at times.

Those that shade those trembling fears,
and those that cover the bare bodied men,
they appear with streams of floating dust,
out of which each was born and raised,
before and after the million steps.
Our skies seem dense with unclear trails,
they attempt to struggle to hold out the sun,
ablaze at times with gleaning streams,
to revert our follies and break the moulds,
or cast afresh a new timeline.

I never looked up so often before,
I never felt the need to stare at the sky,
but something taught me to value the blues,
for its not the ocean that transliterates our tears,
but it is born out of a clear lit sky.

Each day I count the leaves on that tree,
but each time I stop before the last one,

The Skies

I leave it for the day grey clouds appear,
for I know it won't rain each time I am out,
while we walk carefree under the stormy skies.

Since last year I often get up at nights,
or look up each morning before the sunrise,
and the skies appear more strange to me each time.

ON A PLAIN SHEET OF ROLLING SCALES

Have you noticed each dawn is sliding across?
What you had held in your palm last night,
tying it to anew daylight without your consent,
it vanishes amidst the yellow star.
Have you noticed how your face looks today?
It slightly differs from your reflection from last night,
unmoved within your walking thoughts,
it slips you a change amidst the living clock.
Have you noticed that piece you wrote before last sunset?
Now appeals to a lesser number and smells a little stale,
the poem you composed no longer rhymes,
to your thoughts or people it holds.
Each dawn that traverses the days you breathe through,
each new scar that appears on your face,
each thought that you attempt to turn to a verse,
passes by while you were yet to weigh.
Amidst those unrecorded smiles and unheard tales,
it slips by each day each night,
on a plain sheet of rolling scales.

PHOTOGRAPHS

I knew him through a photograph,
one amongst those numerous faces,
that you and I never touched or met.
Those photographs that gave prisms to view,
the unknown ties with unforeseen trails,
that altered me to a more distant self.
From one it grew to several though,
often marked with some resounding names,
I still long to visit those places they hold.
I neither look nor ever delete,
those that never carried a meaning with them,
but my memory fades and the conversations wear off with time.
But, perhaps, his photograph remains.
Those coloured ones that had held a charm,
those negatives and darks that carried his self,
I shall soon delete each one I often decide,
but they remain untouched and no longer suggest,
any sign of his presence or any unsettling thought,
for his photographs were never enough to know him.

WORLDOMETERS

I hear people talking of death these days,
uncertain of the corrections that they need to carve,
in patterns of grief that our cultures hold and sustain.
I see people writing of death,
as they flip through the life cycles of the living,
reduced to the philosophical churnings of the ones who escaped;
Confined to our own interpretation and linkages,
that we impose and superimpose upon the unknown.
I hear people saying that last year was unforeseen,
it taught us new words, new trials, new losses,
irreversible ones that shall never heel.
I often read Donne these days, the metaphysical presence
now turns to a lure of the unseen.
I feel at a loss to find words for my fears,
as each callous musing turns to a dreadful end,
I retire and turn each thought to a question—
do you too check the *worldometers* each morning?

A PAINT BRUSH

When was the last time you dipped
your fingers in a moist soil that drenched
your skin and made it a paint brush with living chords?

As you look through the patterns that cut across the sand particles,
and are drawn to the memories that you have been trying to let go,
you begin to count them upon your brown fingers.

Each time you touch the concrete wall beside which you stand,
you leave marks and patterns of the moist soil,
creating more memories each time you think of the ones you had.

The canvas obliterates each time I begin to paint,
it already has marks that resemble the dried-up soil,
for what once bore life has now turned to a monochrome brush.

DREAMS

Each time I close my eyes and dare to sleep,
I see those dreams that haunt my days,
I see the dead that walk around,
crying in pain and screaming out loud,
I try to call back with a silenced voice.
I see a road beside a lake,
I am running across to reach some place,
unsure I keep circling around,
and none appear upon the crowded scene.
At times I see the flowery pots that I water each day,
turning to tall Eucalyptus trees,
that I never planted in my yard.
I see a child in a fancy cradle,
I see myself calling out to his mom,
she appears nowhere and I see the child
left alone with only me around,
and I abandon him as the cradle falls.
I wake up each time with a tear,
and the dreams continue to haunt.

THE GREEN FLOWER

When I touch the ice below his feet,
upon a desolate ground that is yet to heel,
I tread those scars and an image appears,
I fetch a colour each time to paint,
or attempt to overwrite upon the blank cards
but there is no outline to fill or refill.
With infinities suspending the hope of a spring,
I change the soil each time to start afresh,
or try to fan over the leaves in dark,
but there has not yet been a sign of a green flower.

You and Colours

THE COLOUR WHITE

Do you know there are several shades of the colour white?
They surround me and you in countless hues,
tinged and tarnished.
They elapse in flowing minuscule that stretch around
the thresholds of the colour spectrum.
There is white in the first drop every mother fed the new born,
with a yellow tinge that slowly fades away, and perhaps,
turns invisible as they age.
There is white in the rice puffs whose polished surfaces,
sealed in an expensive packaging,
carefully conceal the brown of the soil.
There is white in the hybrid Rose of York,
no longer a wonder amidst the genetically engineered,
human grown variants that sell at a higher price.
There is a shade of white in every building I visit,
at times however,
they gather men, to pray, to process, to purchase,
to procure the dying as he breathes his last.
I never visited a building devoid of the white.
I see white in the melancholic men that wrap the dead
and conceal the black that the unknown death holds.
There is white that conceals the dead from the world
and draws a veil for the countless grief the men hold.

I often see people abandon the colour white
as they turn fearful,
frantically attempting to colour each part of
the pictures they drew,
for the colour white has proved to be the most frivolous one.
Perhaps, we learnt it from Zeus who
turns white clouds to grey at his will.
I was born in a culture that forbids
the colour white for the brides,
but over time I learnt to appreciate the Chinese bridal gowns.
For me, the colour white represents my outgrowth,
an alienation that I hypocritically endorse.
I know Luna watches us all perplexed each night,
weary, as I say each time, I love
the colour white.

BLUES

Have you seen those countless blues that repeat themselves?
Like that shirt you wore on our last distant call
or in the fancy ink of that pen your drawer holds.
The blue of the bedsheets on woods and soils,
the blue of the pages on shelves and walls,
the blue of the photographs you hated last summer,
and the blue slippers have all vanished alike.
I grew up hating the blue curtains,
and every sister shade of blue was equally charged,
for all blues have held fears for you and me alike.
I am slowly trying to fall in love with the colour blue now,
like the shirt you often repeat this summer,
and the ink you never used for me.

YELLOW

Why was everything so yellow around us?
When you and I began decorating our home,
and I started pasting papers on our apartment walls.
With a highlighter you colored our names in yellow,
and made me listen to the songs on those walls,
like a semi novice learner in your language class.
These days I often reply "yellow"
when asked for my favorite colour,
when I choose not to answer white or pink,
for it appears as a choice alike to two equal dollar bills.
We fell in love with the colour yellow together,
under the yellow lamps in our living room,
that were less bright than your perfumed candles.
The dimmish yellow of the fancy lamps,
the sweeping yellow of the lonely sunsets,
the unreal yellow of the golden dome,
have all painted the imprints of our time together
and this love for the song and the colour called "yellow."

IN SHADES OF LEAVES

Did you know that all leaves have composed a shade card?
To celebrate the fairest one amongst
the mistakenly natural colours,
and the green colour now stands dissected.
With melancholic hierarchies of the young and the old,
and unjust notions of withering away in time,
bracing along the human touch of the dark and the lite.
The parrot green and the olive green,
the emerald green and the pastel green,
the bluish green and the yellowish green,
were all once shades of leaves in a glade from your sketch book.
I have seen towers in green and trees devoid of life,
no longer real like the people and places
that your poems had once created on a colour palate,
ruled by the colour green.

SILVERY

Have you held a silver chain between your fingers?
As it shines as a thread of silvery light,
refracting and reflecting the metallic charm.
The silver plates were never my pick,
the silver foil was never deemed mandatory,
the silver sweets were no longer served,
and silver was slowly fading away without a cause.
I tried to convince you several times
with arguments as long as a breath and a push,
but you refused to love silver and I refused to let you go.
For years I bought and lost several silver rings,
and hid each silver thread under a scarf,
still hoping to convince you someday.

CRIMSON

Why have you always been so fond of the call of the crimson?
As it only stains a part of the whole,
of lives, of living and of love.
It holds a red that painfully appears on ground,
and flows across the densely populated lanes,
often deserted after years of a monarch's rule.
People always loved to paint it in shades of crimson,
as bright as the dawn and as deep as the hell fires,
for contrasting it to the living never bore a cost.
I never saw you in a crimson cloth ever,
and you perhaps had a similar complain,
and we have both been waiting for
the horoscopes to miraculously align.
A crimson carpet and a crimson turban,
a crimson cradle and a crimson flower,
have all been named on the invitation envelopes.
I have been searching a job and saving each penny,
for all the expenses due at the end of the year,
for you and all in the crimson colour.

COLOURS

As they all slowly fell to the ground,
bringing florescent patterns all over and a temperate wind,
the colours were all cast in an artificial spell.
The real ones had been kept in an old Indian closet,
woven over nights that had a silent smell,
with a tapestry of instructions hanging over the clouds.
The colours have always taught us to conform,
to natural ties and untranslatable traits,
but have you ever committed to a colour for a cause?

To them with Love

TO MY MUSE WHO LEFT ME AT THE DELHI AIRPORT

Hai na?
I feel I have come too far from you
To the place you guided me to
Your voice left me when I left the country
Since then, I have been craving to hear you.

Come, let's try the old game once again,
again after answering the same old questions,
yet again visiting the Universal Book Store,
for I know it would have a new stock of the already read pages.
Come, won't you talk again while taking that night walk,
where one can hear the dogs barking from your neighbor's home,
I know the baby won't return,
I perhaps remember him as a Dove now.
Come, for you wanted to live alone,
as you had turned tired of staring at the *Ayurvedic* drugs,
as those bottles threatened you of prolonged quarantines.
Come, for I know you know what I think,
and I know you know that I have always known,
as we started and ended each time with the same question,
hai na?
We can do it all over again

Until we find another question
Come, let's try the old game once again.

Every single poem I wrote was meant for you
Every thought began and ended with you
I have been struggling to find words these days
Come, for I wish to write once again for you.

*Hai na?- A Hindi phrase that translates as "Isn't it so?
*Ayurvedic- Belonging to Ayurveda, the ancient Hindu system of medicine

TO THE NILE IN CAIRO

I have seen you in a photograph, a video and a dream.
Each time your waters were a mix of brown and blue,
each time on a bright summer afternoon,
eternally sunlit and untouched by men.
The stagnant waters in the photograph,
and the walking waves in the video frames,
were cast alive in a dream of Egyptian descent.
I wish to visit you in Cairo alone,
where the photograph, the video and the dream were set,
where your shores come nearest to the Arabian tales I know,
and the winds over you know a familiar touch.
Sometimes I imagine you metamorphosing into Gomti that
flows across my city Lucknow,
but the two rivers are as distant as two scripts,
holding together distinct cultures and life forms within.
Something tells me I will be visiting you next year,
alone in Cairo and beside your busy shores,
to make you a part of my photograph, my video and my dream forever.

TO UNNI IN SEOUL

14 Fischers 1A
was "home" away from our hometowns. You and I,
like a" weird couple" of two crazy women,
became a family for a reason.
Those landscapes and the language lessons,
have translations of life to Korean and Indian formats,
through detours and the dark silent streets, we innocently risked.
Derailing over time under a constant trail,
I often recall saying — "Look at the sky Unni"
as it stretched in picturesque panoramas over two
of a kind and yet distinct,
dreaming often of Prof. Park and Dr. Sharma in a car
driving back to Notre Dame, many years from now.
Everything happened as a part of a plan. Every
mistake happened as a part of the lesson.
We exchanged secrets that none shall know,
trespassing roads without a social sanction,
until the right time.
The innumerable conversations over tea and wine,
the many drives in the South Bend lanes,
the twenty-four hours at the airport together — all
had happened for a reason — all
like a timeline set in a loop.

TO THE LITTLE BLACK CAT

You are the same colour as the door
of the room where you lived as your first human home,
undistinguished between the inverted blankets and eating plates.
You always reminded me of my little baby brother,
who was as tiny as you when I first held his claws,
as blank as you and a dreamless sleep.
I kept talking to you as you kept staring away,
complaining upon the adoption process,
as they handed you over to the wrong father,
in humor, in love, and in a real state.
I told you so much about myself while you were asleep,
for being the imaginary less loved child as you,
though I never had a sibling or a shelter card.
Those sad eyes and scared steps,
those lazy paws and littered lounges,
those hiding places and unused toys,
will always remind me of your presence somewhere.
If we had more time together and if we
had talked more while staring at the lights outside
perhaps, we might have found solutions to ourselves.
I will remember you Fargo for your unloved gaze
and the gift I bought for you on your first birthday
carefully wrapped and safe until I next see you.

TO IFS

For you have been more than a conflict,
a love to the point that I hate to put
into words or verse alike.
You have been a dilemma throughout,
a solution I hate to confess or speak,
with consequences that do not matter.
If I had convinced you to take that trip together,
if you had cared enough not to talk about it,
if we had both stayed indoors on that storm day,
if I had responded well to her advice,
if she had not fallen sick that night,
if he had not broken up just a month ago,
and if all of these 'ifs' had not come true.
The conversations today and yesterday and there after
have altered and aligned to entangled plans
and we now refuse to converse else ways.

TO A FRIEND

I am surprised to see you so well,
with a change of wind and country alike,
you seem happier at home as you prepare to leave.
The past few conversations have been so quick,
as the memory started coming back to me now,
I can feel nothing changed within.
As we still continue to grow distant at times,
as the time still does not matter,
as the unseen sunrise still waits for us,
and as we yet do not know what comes next.
Like a chapter in your favourite novel, and as
an unheard song that I "just add" to my playlist
at times, we try to forget each other,
only to revisit again.

TO MY CONFESSIONS

I have been reading you one after another,
the ones I spoke and ones I hid,
with none that holds the truth in it.
Unposted and unsent drafts,
of him and her and they and all,
with biased blames and complaining calls
of partial thoughts.
I wrote you in a state of loss,
I gave words to you through alien ties,
I do not confess of any truth,
but keep you as those passing tales.

Thought Trails

A BOX OF FUMES

A box of fumes within each frame,
of mortal souls untied to laws,
encased within the falling hopes,
that were once destined to entice your heart.

A handful of mist that each one of us,
carried along the spotless path,
uncovering images of shining domes,
marked upon by the silver stars.

I wrote our names upon each rock,
of luminous screens and flashing slates,
in blacks and whites and thousand fonts,
that morphed along a tenuous carve.

When chaos reverts and timelessness falls,
we shall reach out to unknown lands,
unfolding layers of skies and space,
for then the fumes may drift apart.

A RATIONAL STANCE

We were told of castles and walls lined with men,
of passages that held an effervescent charm,
of gatherings that offered fuel to breaths,
edged along a reverend hand.

We were told of souls that were guarding men,
of leaders who shall rise beyond each fire,
of revolutions that shall lead to coinages that last,
placed in a book with an ancient lock.

We were told of cheers that were destined to transpire,
of eternal rules and inexhaustible laws,
of rains that pour irrespective of seasons,
with a toolbox always held out for all.

Between untold truths and familiar lies,
a layman bridged a passage to nowhere,
with cosmic laws over a No Man's land,
our stories now turn to a rational stance.

NUMB

When the human touch had lost its feel,
to a perpetual cold that embraced within,
in a morbid dusk with a timeless trail,
a residue rests on a shining slate.

The burning frames had left no marks,
the scattered hues no longer seized,
across a lens of refracting poles,
a coded sequence guards each name.

Amidst a storm that holds a voice,
not born out of the phoenix ash,
that failed to turn to a distant form,
a flight conforms to sinking norms.

With breaths turned to lifeless tides,
and silence turned to a deafening scream,
the craving turned to a fearful cry,
and turning numb now grips to heal.

INCOMPLETE

As we complete a circle of incomplete trails,
and return back to straightened roads,
blaming the fates for loops and curves,
we trace footprints on a crowded path.

As we scribble through a page of incomplete thoughts,
and travel back to the first letter on the sheet,
referring to blockages for points of concern,
we forge roadmaps on a map undone.

As we chalk out a melody on an incomplete rhyme,
and route back to the song of an ancient tune,
dismantling rules for a classic stroke,
we succumb to a need of a chosen one.

As we attempt to complete each incomplete trail,
and rework the ways through loss and lure,
speaking out the truth once in a year,
we frame each memory to ensure return.

FOREVER LOST

The time when hours did not count,
with no perplexities of sight and sound,
when salience of joy was rest assured,
and morbid thoughts were never aboard.

When hopes enshrined each sparkling dawn,
and curiosities drove amidst each morn,
to each face was wedded a beautiful smile,
and a motivation rested at the end of each mile.

The cheers now relinquish and the joys perspire,
beneath the burden of each desire,
as the guiding morals no more confine,
scattered in a surreal design.

The memories do revert in solitary hours,
but bring no bliss like the flaxen flowers;
It is 'I' that treads the cost,
for all the times forever lost!

DELUSION

When the mortal mind lost control,
and logic could no more withhold,
the ticking reversed and the clock then broke,
faith withdrew and fears awoke.

A weightless silence then slowly crept on,
screaming out loud-the- tales forlorn,
numbness squirmed, the blood slowly froze,
and the most horrid sounds in the air arose.

The dimensions faded under the scattered skies,
the dying breath had no more sighs.
the senses too now played with mind,
all memories loved were left behind.

All earthly notions were thence denounced,
sanity lost and seclusion pronounced.
the stillness now crowns each rising commotion,
marking the ingress of an eternal delusion.

A JOURNEY OF THOUGHTS

Languid thoughts adrift on a barque,
conceiving dreams in an airy womb,
bouncing on some strange tides,
shall soon give birth to rising hopes.

The sails unfurl on a powerful wind,
and flutter-on the wings of joy,
each thread transforms into a stronger hold,
with woven patterns of blissful hopes.

No nets to stop or lights to guide,
the journey goes on with no plot,
each second announced on its own accord,
and what follow on are novel hopes.

May this journey just go on and on,
the path unbound and wind be strong,
the thoughts may always be afloat,
powered forever by immortal hopes.

She and Her

ORIGINS

When she finally came to terms with love,
with a broken pen and an empty sheet,
the dried-up ink was hard to scan,
but she was writing for an undying strength.

When she finally dreamt to clasp a space,
of unsecure passages and turbulent lanes,
the fears within made a labyrinth map,
but she was walking out of an undying drive.

When she finally awoke to resounding words,
from unknown poets and unfamiliar comrades,
the stagnant waves turned to uncertain forms,
But she was flowing beside undying passions.

She kept searching for these origins within,
but they expanded beyond what her conscious could clasp.
Earth was her strength
Fire bore her drive
Water immersed her passions
And then her thoughts were the wind.

DAYS

There are days when she is sinking within
There are days when days refuse to lift her
There are days when she tries her best to conform
There are other days when things appear perfectly imperfect
There are days that bring hopes of travel
There are days when she is planning a call
And days when calls make her regret the loss
There are days when she talks to him and her
There are days when time tests her bad
There are days when all things fall apart
And there are days when those pieces align to a start.

WOMEN

I have met several women so far.
their images intact in my memory,
their words resonating.
I remember each one,
but none of the memories overlap.
I have met several women.
One of them in her early twenties,
as fragile as her thoughts,
she now lives alone in a new city,
I remember her as the stronger one now.
Another of them in her thirties,
refuses to marry for the people around,
she works alone and runs her family now.
There were several others,
in their forties, fifties and sixties,
and they were not at all alike as most claim.
They carry different shades to their bodies,
clasped in differing roles and strengths,
yet similar in ways within.
They do not turn to men to lean on,
they do not shatter beneath what life threw,
they do not stop for a reason as they say,
for being a woman was at least never one.
Perhaps, I wish to meet more of such women often.

CLICHED

An often instance now remains,
your clichéd view of 'Her' and
'each' type of 'that' girl,
marked by the shade of her lipstick,
by the wink of her eye,
by the way she speaks,
or denies a call or clasps to a sigh.
As she rushes to a door,
or turns away at a voice,
she holds it within,
or returns it with a smile.
For she loses herself each time she conforms,
there's more to 'Her' than her being a 'woman'
more to 'Her' than what the pronouns denote,
much remains unresolved within the ideals that entrap,
to unravel beyond her clichéd 'womanhood.'

CAGED

I had been searching your marks as I turned each page,
you had possessed me like a caged bird,
with each step we were moving apart,
but you continued to lead me through.

I was awaiting your words as I heard each friend,
your answers seemed to pierce each call,
with each word I moved ahead and alone,
but your absence matters no more.

Like an ancient myth,
I believe in your words,
I am the *Shakti,*
I sustain each blow,
I rise out of each fear,
and I shall turn each cage to spaces afloat,
perhaps even you.

*Shakti- A Hindi word meaning power

SHE

Now with each step, she looks around
and at every turn, she stops to glance.
She suspects each face,
turns at each similar voice,
and her sight now follows each passing touch.

"Why are you being afraid of him?" they asked
"That happens with every other girl in our nation" they consoled
"He's not following you any longer!" they affirmed
"Be brave and learn to be bold" she heard.
She found herself devoid of words,
to explain herself or each one around,
what had passed by in events or days,
with him or her and now the rest.

Each statement passed,
each doubtful glance,
each question asked,
each suggestion made,
now is a part of her memory.

It was not her fear but her failure to retort,
it was not her mistake but her inability to foresee,
it was not uncommon yet a shiver passed.
now each time she recalls the day,
and attempts to chalk out an alternate path,
each conversation echoes inside her head,
she sinks within yet walks ahead.

FOR OMNIA VINCIT AMOR

Before the spring ends this year,
I intended to confess my love to him.

As April appears again,
I wonder if you could be mine ever.
Unlike Radha, I cannot be your beloved
Unlike Aurora, I can never get you the immortal boon
but you never take these names as we talk.
As a new year begins this month,
I wonder if I could be yours ever.
Unlike Sita, I cannot tie my life to one
Unlike Helen, I cannot bring you to an end
but you never mention these names as you write.
As past reverts and present unfolds,
these names turn and enclose each knot,
I strive to fetch you against my will,
but you remain unmoved by each.

As summer begins in India and shall soon drift by,
I shall perhaps confess my love to him next spring.

*Radha- A milkmaid who is described as the beloved and chief consort of God Krishna in the Hindu epic *Mahabbharata.*
*Aurora- The Goddess of Dawn in Roman mythology who had a mortal lover named Tithonus for whom she asked Jupiter for the boon of immortality but forgot to ask for immortal youth.
*Sita- One of the central figures in the Hindu epic *Ramayana* who is the wife of God Rama and is worshipped as an ideal wife.
*Helen- In Greek mythology, Helen is the most beautiful woman in the world whose abduction by Paris leads to the Trojan War.

Set on a Stage

DAD

Prologue

Perhaps, someday…
I would describe my Mom in an epic,
I would dedicate all my songs to my love,
I would critique the social cause at length,
and attempt to weave my life into words.
I would try to recall those forgotten names in print,
I would formally thank each one in my list,
I would write a line for each one I ever met,
But Dad, for you I would never attempt one.

There is no 'one' scene today to describe in words
No action for which a pen could suffice
On a sheet of paper or a shining screen
On which I could sketch out his life.

For every man who raised a daughter
Empowered her enough to have a voice
Educated her enough to express in words
Deserves more words than I could write.

There can possibly be no *Epilogue* yet
For I am still writing this song
For you and me and our fathers still
Who continue to live or reside in our hearts…

AN ALTERNATE WORLD

Prologue

It had not always been such a delirium
It grew out of a frantic search
It breathes in patterns of ekphrastic turns.

Scene I

There have been leaves scattered all around
The clouds steaming low
The waters stagnant and blue
Everything appears in unrealistic natural hues

Scene II

There has always been a line of descent
That now stands disrupted by a new perception
There is a new desire born out of the remapping,
Short and un-swift
Aging yet un-moved
Scared yet un-tarnished

Scene III

Lately, it had been rearranging the set descriptions.
Lately, it had been stepping out of the pre-built spaces.

Lately, it had been slowly reconfiguring the locale.
A change of plans now threatens the status-co.

Epilogue

But yet tracing each move,
But yet figuring out away,
But yet circling back to square one.
Unpredictable,
This world offers no signs.

LOVE

Prologue

Your confessions never mattered
Your agreement was never my call
Your choices never governed mine
Your confusions were born out of your own mind
Your perfection was never my necessity
Your insecurities were never my concern
Your impatience was not my drive
Your anger was not fueling my life
Your comfort was never my hope
Your peace was not a part of my shopping list
Your charm never made me insecure
Your happiness was always yours

Scene I

Something tells me it might possibly be a dream
It shall be over with a wink
With nothing changed

Scene II

There is a new word we learnt— 'quarantine'— and the
television news now begins to alarm

But I have stumbled upon your 'presence' somehow
Now it's a newer world within a changing time

Scene III

The possibilities of an end finally liberate me from my fears
And I dare to embrace you in my thoughts
For I know we would never step out of our houses and ever meet

Scene IV

Your voice is enough to calm my nerves
Your smile is enough to take me to mine
Your presence within my smartphone suffices my quarantine

Epilogue

With no promises of future
Escaping the dreads of the present time
The most beautiful of its kind was perhaps
An encounter with love in the times of quarantine

AFTER YEARS I TURN TO INK

Prologue

It has been a decade
Since I last wrote a song
Or heard a voice that could pierce
This hauntingly silent calm.

Each time he paints a word-full note
Each time he weaves a latent line
Each time he carves an unknown site
Each time he despairs the lonely tides
Each time he breaks the silent storms
Each time he questions the unheard call
Each time he wows for the unseen ties
Each time he answers that unexpected sigh
Each time he travels to those un-inhabited lands
Each time he drowns in those flowing streams
Each time he lights a darkened lamp
Each time he turns to distant dreams
Each time he turns his thoughts to words
Each time he types from right to left
Each time he speaks in that foreign tongue
The words are lost but echoes heard

Epilogue

He takes me back to those unlocked doors
That I never dared to wander past
But now my verses turn to life, and
After years I turn to ink

AN ENCOUNTER WITH AN ANGEL

Prologue

I had been hearing him for so long
Discontinuous
I had been scrolling his past words
With brackets
I had been sure of his unnatural non-existence
But perhaps incorrectly

Act I

As I was erasing my poems
The constant use of a singularity of vowels
I saw him sitting next to me with the yellow diary
Reading out loud the lines I had already erased
I minimized the document and switched back to reading.

Act II

I could hear him reading my last poem
We do not have angels back home
I turned around to tell him
They do not read poems
He went on to read the second last one I erased

Act III

He spoke nothing
Blankly staring at the white pages from which he read

He left as I began to type the title of my new document
Tathastu: An Encounter with an Angel…
I had been hearing him for so long,
Discontinuous,

Act IV

Appearing and Disappearing
The words kept coming back to me
In fragments
In episodes
As he appeared and could be heard
For oblivion
For memory
Wearing a green ink aroma
I could barely read the characters printed all over his body
He was made of my floating thoughts
Each part of his human shaped body reminded me of an episode
Each time I tried to read him he grew dense

Epilogue

Between memory and oblivion
Between remembrance and escape
Between relapse and recovery
I had been struggling to erase every other name

*Tathastu- A Sanskrit word that translates as "So Be It" and is found in Hindu mythology as the phrase spoken by a deity to grant a wish

MOTHERHOOD

Prologue

A salute to every mom, yours and mine
who chose to be one
out of love or fate.
In introspect I cannot ever agree
to become one in post 'you and me.'

Interlude

I need your presence but not your power
I hold your views but not your command
I indulge in your fancies but not your flaws
I succumb to your hopes but not your thoughts
I attempt to make you smile but not beyond my worth
I feel loved by your care but do not wish to depend
I would love to see you fly but I cannot promise my pace
I hope you get there but without redefining this state
I feel anxious by your silence but choose not to revert
I do fall for your longing but dilute the urge
I am flawed and broken but you erased it for a while
I chose your love but you preferred the social ties
I was reluctant to promise but you still managed for a while
I know I made it difficult but it was meant to resolve with time

The Skies

I often try to forget but you left me with an altered life
I wish you had stayed on but perhaps, I had left you no choice

Epilogue

When I said "No" to motherhood and you did not disagree
But changed the subject to more flexible lines
I wish you had stayed and showed a mirror to my fears
Like you had done each time before when I refused to care

YOU WALK IN MY WORDS

Prologue

This is not a true story
Do not mistake the 'I' for the real me
For once in a while it happens
You read what you were never meant to read

Scene I

These empty white sheets now begin to haunt
Each time the silence falls
You convinced me I could never hold the pen again

Scene II

How could you still manage to write?
And I know we will write for the rest of our lives
But the reasons have changed for you and me

Scene III

It fades away they say
After a year or so
But I pray that you leave my words too

Scene IV

It's been a decade now
I have been reading you like the Bible since
I only follow but somehow always fail to interpret you

Epilogue

This is not an imaginary tale
Do not mistake the 'you' for unreal names,
For not just once but always
You know you walk in my words too.

Within

I

I try to be you,
in words,
in thoughts,
in voice.

I attempt imitations,
of love,
of cheer,
of life.

I respond unwillingly
to care,
to work,
to all I know.

I am trapped
bnetween you and me,
I am no more like me,
no more like you,
ever enough for either,
I am just what I could be,
just I.

FROM 17 TO 27

I fail to recall the past decade.
The events that passed,
the people I met,
and the days that I crossed across this timeline.
I try to search in my own records,
in photographs and books,
that I had clicked or saved,
I return each time to an empty space.
The countless smiles or the shady hopes,
I wander how and when I spent,
those riddles torn and spaces left,
as it all now sums up to a decade lost.

A CHOICE

I was never asked a choice
within the branding ceremony
that left me an altered self
not for a day or two
but a lifetime.
They said that it was irreversible
And it's just the fate that plays out
humans succumb to medical laws
and you are never offered a choice.

But something changed that was
Not material in its specific sense
She just said a word and I healed
Beyond the images of the disability curse
And perhaps it was not a word but
A phrase
A statement
A call
Or just a query,
I will never forget the day she asked
"Disabled?"
And gave me the choice of a "no."

ORIENTALIST

I think in a foreign tongue,
beyond the pre-linguistic descent,
out of the genetic codes to packaged boxes,
from one choice to another,
I wish to be called an Orientalist.

A SEARCH

He left with a proverb
That I could not decode
In unconscious attempts
I searched those texts.

He left with a poem
That I failed to detest
In vain I read it over
As I searched for a mistake.

He left with multiple goodbyes
That I struggled to believe
In seclusion and retrospect
I searched for my disbelief.

Each word holds an echo
And memories unearth
Beyond his real presence
As I still continue to search

ILLUSIONS OF YOUR PRESENCE

Ten years back, or perhaps more—
you told me that story— I was a child— an ignorant one-
I remember each word-it surprises me at times—
Your voice— that can never be heard again.

An unknown horror clasps my thoughts—
an untold fear—
I begin to recall the story word by word—
I fear—
what if my memory fails me some day?
I haven't overcome the fear of penning it down yet.

The story is the hope- your memory—
your presence—
a chant, a mantra, a recalling.

time has changed all that was yours—
no traces of your life linger—
no signs of the past to hold on to—
but the story remains- within my thoughts—
and it suffices all that I need
for creating—
illusions of your presence.

INDIAN ALLAMANDA

Have you counted the petals in yellow
That imperfectly align between your fingers
For they have been molded in an invisible cast

Last night, several hours before the sunrise,
I stood with my face closely pressed along the metallic net, staring,
at nothing. None stood out in the dark.
As the cold wind brushed across my face,
carrying out the *Manokamini* fragrance that stands in full bloom,
I struggled to find a reason to stay on.

Have you carefully crushed the singular petal
That refrains to leave a yellow stain
For your skin appear as a plastic foil to them

The wind outside grew heavier, stormy,
it would be a rainy morning soon,
with heavy clouds across a panorama,
of nothingness. Unwritten manuscripts that lay,
on my study table in the next room, remind me of the
resonating nothingness.

There was no storm last night,
I walk out and stand next to the *Manokamin*i tree,
And recall *Allamanda*, from the dream last night.

Note: *Manokamini* is a native South-Asian shrub with white or cream flowers.

Journeys

DUST SKETCHES

The dust had been poured out in a perfume bottle,
the one I had been searching for him.

Last April I flipped through the magic chronicle,
and placed a bookmark with my name upon a map,
I had never traveled to another city alone.
The days, the weeks, and the months last year,
were sprinkled by his altering presence,
I never saw him mending the color of the roads.

The journey,
the yellow leaves,
the hut shaped houses,
the sunlight around 8 pm,
the church bells at the university chapel,
had all been sketched last summer by the dust,
before it was carefully poured out in the perfume bottle,
the one he had chosen for me.

A LETTER

Dear poet friend,
How is everything back home?
You remember it had been last August
when, you had been writing to me so often
and, asking me to prepare for the journey
while, making me relearn my mother tongue again,
I had fallen in love with your poetry,
and the only way to be with you was to be away.
I never saw it rain here for more than fifty seconds,
and the sun appears longer than the Indian days,
but I wish to tell you more than the sky strokes,
and I won't be writing to you again until it snows.
Cooking all the wrong recipes,
buying all the wrong pieces for the jigsaw,
condensing all the wrong alleys,
borrowing all the incorrect places,
just as it was last August, I am
and wish to always stay,
your constant reader.
August 2021

DISCOVERY

In the south west corner of the city
 they had mapped, a long-silenced protest.
Just adjacent to the spot the martyrs lay
with their combustible profundity, shattered dead
across the alley to the sacred unearthed graves.
Thirteen had been crossed out as a superstition,
just a day before the journey started,
left aligned to the outdoor panoramas.
They knew it was a mistake of the viewing points,
yet with a perfectly laid out sequence,
the map had been a detour to the discovery.

NORTHERN LIGHTS

I wish to visit Norway once,
during winters, on a December night,
to witness the Northern Lights.
I have visited it several times in a dream,
where I stand below the green lit sky,
and dancing streams of florescent hues,
crisscross across the Arctic skies.
I see many familiar smiles around,
staring at the sky with their cameras,
as the lights transcend.
I plan a travel to Norway each year,
and each year I lose a friend.

THE CONCEALED SKYLINE

As he knelt down at the threshold that separated the two worlds,
they promised to return him to his lost fates.
He was born to be a King,
their sunlit faces eclipsing his love for Hercules,
slowly enticing him to their waters,
where human forms and mortal breaths sink,
where the sapphires engulf the sepia.
The skies had been bright that day,
but perhaps they were concealed as an anti-symbolic dogma.
Hylas was about to be lost forever,
concealing the conspiracies of the clear skyline,
concealing the horizons that the Argo was yet to tread.
He, still kneeling at the threshold,
they, still singing out the promises,
as the voyage froze upon the Fates that were yet to follow,
but even today, Jupiter continues to silently stare at the nymphs,
still waiting, upon the concealed skyline.

NOWHERE

The confessions of love and illusions of hope
The decisions to move and prescriptions to lose,
The truths that stumble and the mockeries that affirm,
Between passages that dictate and promises of return,
To erase each mark and to undo each turn
Reconfiguring each memory and reworking each one.
A search that wanders in a loop and threatens to despair
With a hand held out and takes one to a nowhere.

VENTRILOQUIST

I wake up around each midnight, to hear
her humming, resembling a distressed call to an unknown comrade.

I know she sits on a tall branch, not very far
upon the Golden Shower tree, from the last poem we wrote together.
The miles she flew, unguided at nights, resound through the
temporary walls.
I had been thinking of a name, my insomnia grows as
she sings unnaturally at night, like a dismayed ventriloquist.

Abstractions

THE COLOUR SPECTRUM

The colour spectrum that had several shades
of you
slowly obliterates
as the words refuse to conform to the shades
slowly conjures
as the shades refuse to conform to the canvas
slowly reformulates
as the canvas refuses to conform to the frame
slowly melts
as the frame refuses to conform to the conscience
slowly adapts
as the conscience refuses to conform to the change
slowly readjusts
as the color spectrum now has all the distinct shades
of men and women alike.

PATTERNS

The delirium continues
to haunt within a changing
world of trails and thoughts.

The presets in a cage are,
half broken.
The paradigms in a nutshell are,
half established.
The possibilities of a calm are,
half calculated.

Now,
it counts backwards in dates and times.
Now,
it spills and trips the empty jars.
Now,
it attempts to grasp it all over again.

SEVERAL-S

From several to several-s,
non-existing yet a new interjection,
they appear and disappear in momentary thoughts.
Too many at times.
Convoluted in words.
Prescribed.
The idea of the new
 has always been
the problem.
It has grown from several to several-s now.

A PERFORMANCE

There was an urgent need to correct the shades,
it had been troubling them both since its inception.
The series of experimentations,
the prisms that had fallen dead,
those countless that had been lost
to the green air. All had to be stopped.
There had been speculations each day,
and it had to culminate now.
He finally stretched out his palm to perform
the rites, the act was to be staged.
She metamorphosed into a figure and a shade,
and they were finally ready for the performance.
There was something odd about the directions,
an unusual heaviness upon the stance.
There were two minds now,
two splits to measure the heights.
One closer to a human form,
another closer to the human need.

SYNCHRONY

The feminine bodies aligned in perfect synchrony,
with music cast as a spell upon their minds,
the two paused for a moment, only to continue again.

None could divorce the rhythm from their expressions,
the sensual touch they imitated,
the enchanting gestures of an indigenous origin.

Their hair tied back,
their bodies ornamented with metallic crafts,
their costumes bearing the same cuts in different colours,
their faces decorated alike,
as the two performed in a trance.

The Asian melody alternated with their breaths,
turning their faces away, in an embrace,
they paused, to be framed forever.

THE CHAOS

They gifted an illusion
of a perpetual calm
to mended minds.

They dictated a blessing
upon the empty hands
with naked cries.

They converted the myths
of hungry dogs to men
with golden plates.

They created a rift
between the crux of hopes
across the towers.

They empowered the disabled
but once in a decade perhaps
for exceptions' sake.

They replaced it all
by a deafening void
of the chaos.

REASSEMBLED

A screen
A letter
A note
A noise
And a mind that wrestles.

A thought
A promise
A chance
A hope
And a heart that wrestles.

A touch
A kiss
A hand
A breath
And a fate that wrestles.

PRODIGY

In parenthesis, often hyphenated, or broken apart,
constructed upon incongruous orders,
experimentations with the edifice were proofread by her.
In calculative time zones, un-intoxicated,
the form had to be intentionally incompatible,
unmeaning, each time read over a microphone.
The delirium was phased,
and the corrections were industrially disciplined,
spaced, yet conjoined.
In pleasing patterns that un-sustain,
the manuscript was conditioned to be volatile,
typed, yet unreadable.
She had been writing it over for a year now,
the prodigy had been promising,
uncertain, eclectic and (re-correct-ed).

CREATIONS

Musings
with
you and colours
written
to them with love
in
thought trails
on
she and her
once
set on the stage
and
within
for
journeys
across
abstractions
under
the skies.

PUBLICATION CREDITS

"Dust Sketches." *Pixie Dust & All Things Magical: Global Poetry in English 2022,* edited by Anita Nahal, Authorspress, 23 January 2022, ASIN B09R2DRYBS.

"To my muse who left me at the Delhi airport." *Teesta Review: A Journal of Poetry*, vol. 4, no. 2. November 2021. ISSN: 2581-7094.

"The Colour White," "Worldometers," and "A Paint Brush." *The Quiver Review*, 18 May 2021.

"The Skies," "Dreams," "The Green Flower." *Lothlorien Poetry Journal*, 13 May 2021.

"On a plain sheet of rolling scales," "She," "Photographs." *Setu Bilingual* monthly journal, April 2021.

"For For *Omnia vincit amor"* and "A Rational Stance." *Aspiring Writers Society E-zine,* April 2021.

"Women." *Rhetorica Quarterly*. March 2020.

"Origins." *Earth, Fire, Water, Wind: An Anthology of Poems*, edited by Anita Naha and Roopali Sircar Gaur, ASIN : B08X244V8G, Authorspress, 18 February 2021.

"Numb." *Trouville Review,* 16 October 2020. by.

“After Years I turn to ink.” *Confluence: South Asian Perspectives,* August 2020, ISSN: 2633-4704.

“A Box of Fumes” and “The Chaos.” *Café Dissensus Everyday,* 8 June 2020.

“Love.” *Borderless*, 25 May 2020.

“Delusion.” *GNOSIS- An International Refereed Journal of English Language and Literature*, vol. 4, no. 4, July 2018, ISSN 2394-0131

“A Journey of Thoughts.” *The Criterion, An International Journal in English,* vol. 8, no. 6, December 2017.

“Forever Lost.” *Ashvamegh, Indian Journal of English Literature,* Issue 18, July 2016, ISSN: 2454-4574.

www.ingramcontent.com/pod-product-compliance
Lightning Source LLC
LaVergne TN
LVHW041117150826
845673LV00007B/2098

* 9 7 8 9 3 9 1 4 3 1 1 0 5 *